I0457341

THE GEORGIAN SYNAXARIUM

Translated by: D.P. Curtin

Dalcassian
Publishing
Company
PHILADELPHIA, PA

Copyright @ 2022 Dalcassian Publishing Company

All rights reserved. No part of this publication may be reproduced, distributed, or transmitted in any form or by any means, including photocopying, recording, or other electronic or mechanical methods, without the prior written permission of the publisher, except in the case of brief quotations embodied in critical reviews and certain other non-commercial uses permitted by copyright law. For permission request, write to Dalcassian Publishing Company at dalcassianpublishing at gmail.com

ISBN: 978-1-960069-69-6 (Paperback)

Library of Congress Control Number:
Author: Curtin, D.P. (1985-)

Front cover image: Orthodox Icon of St. George the Victorious and the Dragon (rus. Икона Святой Георгий Победоносец и дракон)
Book design by J.J. Ripplestick

Printed by Ingram Content Group, 1 Ingram Blvd, La Vergne, Tennessee

First printing edition 2023.

FORWARD

This text is a reproduced work found only in Georgian, from the Monastery of Iviron, on the peninsula of Mt. Athos in Greece. The author, a priest named Lucian, appears to relate events that have transpired within the Roman Empire during the reigns of Theodosius II and Constantine III. It would be a vast oversimplification to assume that this was the antiquity of the document itself. Its original scholar, Nikolai Marr, who translated the work from Georgian into French, believed it to be a work of the 10th century based upon the reading of this unique text. While there are a plethora of Georgian synaxarium, this one is unique in both the voice of its narration, and also its fragmentary composition. What survives appears to be a composite text, perhaps containing some small elements of the 5th century, but more likely compiled during the height of Byzantine academia during the Macedonian dynasty. Our author certainly seems familiar with the imperial system of indiction. That is to say, the ordering of years into a broader epoch of fifteen years. This chronological system was in play from the reign of Constantine the first, until well after the empire was dissolved into Ottoman suzerainty in the 16th century. Based upon the transposition of the manuscript, its antiquity must pre-date that date given by Marr by at least a few centuries, as its composition appears to be in the Monastery of St. Saba in Jerusalem, during the late 9th century. A similar document has been found within the famous library of St. Catherine's monastery at the foot of Mt. Sinai. However, this fellow document also appears to be missing sections, and is either a copy of this work, or is drawn from an identical parent-document.

This synaxarium grants some insight into the Georgian perspective of the early church, albeit one that is profoundly influenced by the broader Byzantine cultural commonwealth. Its hagiographies impart some otherwise forgotten tradition of the lives of the saints that were salient to the early community of the Georgian church and might grant us insight into the cultural legacy of Georgian Monasticism specifically.

D.P. Curtin
Johnstown, PA
July 7, 2022

CHRIST
IN THE NAME OF GOD
THE COLLECTION OF THE BOOK IS LAID OUT AS FOLLOWS:
THE 27th DAY OF DECEMBER: STEPHEN

1st chapter. The Martyrdom of Saint Stephen.

2nd— The discovery of the relics of Stephen.

3rd— The return of Stephen's relics.

4th— The sermon of Gregory the priest on Stephen.

5th— The eulogy of Stephen by the same Gregory the priest.

6th— The commemoration of Peter and Paul.

7th— The martyrdom of the apostle Paul.

8th— The martyrdom of Peter and Paul.

10th— The life of Dionysius.

11th— The Epistle of Dionysius.

12th— The martyrdom of the apostle James, brother of the Lord.

13th— The martyrdom of Saint Basil of Ham.

14th— The martyrdom of Saint Habo.

15th— The baptism of Saint Habo.

16th— The Martyrdom of the Same Saint Habo.

17th— Praise of Saint Habo.

18th— The life of the fathers of Sinai.

19th— (The Martyrdom) of Saint Babila.

20th— The Martyrdom of Saint Anthony Ravakh.

21st— The Martyrdom of Saints Speusippus, Eleusippus, and Meleusippus.

22nd— The martyrdom of Saint Timothy and Saint Moor

23rd— The martyrdom of the apostle Timothy.

24th— The Martyrdom of Cyre and John.

25th— The Martyrdom of Saint Boa.

26th— The Martyrdom of Saint Eusegne.

27th— The Martyrdom of Saint Julian of Emesa.

28th— The Life of Saint Theodore.

29th— The Martyrdom of Saint Theodore.

30th— The Life of Saint Euphrosyne.

31st— [The acts] of nine holy brothers of Cola.

32nd— The Martyrdom of Saint David of Douin.

33rd— The Martyrdom of Saint Julian.

34th— The martyrdom of the forty saints

35th— The eulogy of the forty saints.

36th— The martyrdom of Saint Phileetamin.

37th— The Martyrdom of Saint Michael the Monk.

38th— The Martyrdom of Saint Vardan.

39th— The Martyrdom of Saint Atom.

40th— The Martyrdom of the Saints of Soucave.

41st— The Death of Saint Isaac the Parthian (Partheve) ("The Fulfillmentment").

42nd— (The martyrdom) of the holy queen Chouchanic.

43rd— (The Martyrdom) of Izidbozid.

44th— The Martyrdom of Aristaques.

45th— The Martyrdom of Saint George.

46th— Praise of Saint George.

47th— The Martyrdom of Saint Longinus the Genturion.

48th— The Martyrdom of Saint Mark the Evangelist.

49th— (The acts) of Saint Roman the New Martyr.

50th— The martyrdom of the holy queen Senedoukhte.

51st— The martyrdom of Saint Philemon the torch player.

52nd— (The Martyrdom) of Saints David and Tiritchane.

53rd— The Martyrdom of Saint Thalele.

54th— The martyrdom of Saint Cyprian.

55th— The martyrdom of Saint Christopher.

56th— The martyrdom of Saint Conon

57th— The martyrdom of Saint Leontius.

58th— The martyrdom of Saint Mama.

59th— The martyrdom of Saint Phocas.

60th— The martyrdom of Saint Jusique.

61st— The martyrdom of Saint George the Zoravar.

62nd— The martyrdom of Saint Nerse the Archbishop.

63rd— The martyrdom of Saint Goulandoukhte.

64th— The martyrdom of Saints Tracus, Probe and Andronicus.

I. — THE MARTYRDOM OF SAINT STEPHEN

[...] I saw the chariot of fire and I noticed St. Stephen sitting there and so he was taken up to Our Lord Jesus Christ, who returns honor and glory from century to century. Amen.

II. — THE DISCOVERY OF THE RELICS OF SAINT STEPHEN, FIRST DEACON AND FIRST MARTYR.

You who are holy and servants of God in towns and villages. You who are valorous, bishops and priests together with all the believers of Christ Jesus, servants of the churches, and the fathers, anchorites, I greet you, by the Lord, I, Lucian the wretched and most reprobate.

God, Benefactor and Philanthropist, wanted to raise the horn of his Anointed. That is to say the preaching of the Gospel. He wanted to reveal through me, to the poor, in the last days of the holy servants, the archdeacon and first martyr Stephen. He is thrice blessed and glorified, who saw with his own eyes the King of heaven, as well as Nicodemus who in the Gospel called, from good memory, blessed; and Gamaliel who is praised in the Acts of the Apostles for his goodwill as worthy of thanks, and above all to his son Abibus, of whom there is no mention in Scripture. However, he is glorified independently of the Scripture, along with a number of saints, before God, as it appeared to my unworthy self, in the three kinds of revelation, and hearing this, it helps me through your holy prayers, to glorify God who confers such a revelation, a grace on sinners, of whom I am the first.

The mode of revelation is as follows: I fell asleep, as I was accustomed before, in the distant baptistery, where there was a chest in which one puts the utensils of the church. Friday was about to dawn, in the month of April, the third day, at the dawn of the fifteenth, at the tenth consulship, the sixth year of our crowned master, Theodosius the monarch.

At the third hour of the night, being still awake, as something struck me, I was dismayed and I saw a tall and aged man, of admirable beauty. He had been wrapped in a white shroud, and at the four corners of the shroud had been put pieces, cloths of gold, and under each of these pieces was placed an image of the cross of the Lord, the color of gold. He was wearing sandals with golden straps; he held the golden star in his right hand. He came to me and, standing beside me, struck me with his backhand three times, and called my name three times. And I answered him: "What is it, lord? And he said to me, "Go up to Jerusalem and tell the holy bishop: 'How long will we be hidden and how long will you not discover us and let everyone know our bravery. For it is fitting that people come to the hour of your archpriests, discovering them as quickly as possible. That door of human love may be opened, through us, to the world, because it is plunged in anxiety and draws near to perdition, because of the multitude of iniquities that are committed there daily. Such care is necessary not only for me alone, but even more for those who are close to me, they are worthy of many honors and glory. The place of our burial is uncultivated, and our bones sometimes get wet from the rain, and again comes the time when they dry out in the sun. Our bones are diminishing, day by day, because the unworthy are trampling upon us". And I, Lucien the poor, answered him, and said: "Who are you, sir, or who are those who are with you, or in what place can we find you?"

He said: "I am Gamaliel, the same person who raised Paul and made him Doctor of the Law in Jerusalem. As for those who are buried with me, it is my lord himself, it is Stephen, who was stoned to death by the infidel Jews in Jerusalem. And they cast him into the way outside the city gates to the north, and there he lay all day and all night. Since the high priests, being faithless, issued the order that no one bury him and that he was left to be devoured by the beasts and torn by the birds. I, Gamaliel, knew of his courage, and wished to share in the faith in the days of the resurrection. I rose secretly in the night and called the men whom I knew as saints and as believers in Christ, and who had just taken the light. I made them understand, I informed them and I instructed them to go and take the body of Stephen, according to my order, and to carry it to my estate which is called, after my name, Capar-Gamal, which is only twenty miles from the city. They performed this rite of quarantine there, according to the regulations of the law, and I gave the order to provide the mourners with everything they needed, at the expense of my township. So they buried him in my new sepulcher, where no one had yet laid them."

"Now he who is buried with him is Nicodemus, my father's brother, the same man who came in the night to our Savior Jesus, and was instructed by Him, believing that it was necessary to be born again by water and by the Holy Spirit. He took the light through Peter, one of his disciples."

"As soon as the archpriests and the Pharisees heard, they got angry and thought of killing him, following the example of Saint Stephen. However, they did not dare to kill him, out of respect for me, since they knew that he was related to me, but they anathematized him. They deprived him of the dignity of leadership, took away his wealth, beat him with terrible blows, covered him with wounds and expelled him from the city."

"Now I, Gamaliel, took him also, in secret, to my village, where Lucian was a priest. I assigned him his daily portion of my wealth. Shortly thereafter, he died, and he too rested, as confessor of Christ. I gave orders to bury him at the feet of Saint Stephen. Finally, the third who is buried with us is Abiba, my beloved younger son. He and I took the light, through the intermediary of the same disciples, who were disciples of the Savior. it is the one who, in Judaism, was called 'Adda'. When he took the light, he was given the name of Sakuarel [Agape], which is said in Syriac as 'Abiba'".

"He was, for twenty years, a disciple of the law more than I was and took instruction with Paul in the Temple. He had no engagement with the female sex, he looked at no woman except his mother, and he died immaculate and undefiled. It was then that by following him, that I, Gamaliel, ended my days and buried me near my son in the tomb above Stephen. Now my wife, Edana, and my firstborn son, Selemia, instead of adhering to the faith of Christ, brought up a new persecution against me, because we had accepted the light, they separated themselves from us and went away."

We set out and arrived in the village of my mother, which is called Kepar-Selemia. He left this world there and was not worthy to be buried with us in the tomb. So I, Lucian, got up the same night, gave thanks to the Lord and fulfilled my prayer to God by saying: "God, Eternal Lord, if this vision came to me through your love of man, order that it be revealed to me a second and a third time."

I began fasting and praying to forty saints of old. During the night of the following Friday, at the same hour, Gamaliel came as he had first appeared to me, and remained standing near me, he said to me: "Why have you been negligent, and you have not gone up to Bishop John to tell him what I had told you?"

I answered him thus: "Pardon me, lord, but having been warned by the vision only once, I did not have the courage to move such an Archpriest of God , because I knew from the divine books that everything must be confirmed by the account of two or three witnesses."

Thereafter I dared to say to myself: "If this vision which I have seen is from the Lord, may he agree to reveal it a second time and even a third time. Now rejoice, therefore, as second recurring apparition, even a third appearance, so that it may be ascertained."

Then he raised his voice, stretched out his hand and pronounced three times: "Your sin is forgiven!"

And when he was about to pass the door, he stopped a little, turned around and said to me: "Look at me, priest, stop to say another thing".

I replied, "What is it, lord?"

And he said to me: "I know that doubt has invaded you and that you have said to yourself in your heart: 'If this happens, and if we find all the four together in the tomb, how will I manage to recognize the relics of Saint Stephen?' It is not what you think. The burial of each of us is plainly visible".

And I said to him, "How is it, lord?"

And he said to me: "Leave in your heart all the images that I will show you." He stretched out his hands, and I saw four baskets, three gold and one silver. The gold ones were full of roses, two of them with white roses and the third with blood-red roses. The silver one was full of aromatic lilies and was attached to one of the gold baskets. Both of these appeared above the others. The basket filled with red roses stood on my right on the east side, while those filled with white roses and the single basket filled with lilies stood on my left on the north side.

Now, two baskets suspended in the air rose from the ground only three cubits. He then said to me: "Have you seen these baskets?"
"Yes, sir," I replied.

He went on: "The baskets are the graves of our bones and the basket full of red roses is that of lord Stephen. For he is the only martyr who came to join us. The basket that you see straight ahead is Nicodemus, confessor of Christ. The baskets suspended in the air that you see lifted from the ground are me and my son."

I took the liberty to ask him: "Lord, why is one of these two baskets gold and the other silver? And why is one full of red roses and the other full of lilies."
"The silver basket," he said to me, "is the burial place of my son, because he was chaste in body and shone with his spirit like silver. He had been brought up in the temple of God and had never looked at a woman except his mother. That is why this basket is full of lilies".

I immediately gave thanks to the man of God and waited for his arrival for the third time. On the third Friday Gamaliel came at the same time, stood before me face to face, admirable as he was, and in a voice of anger said to me: "What are you thinking? Why this indolence? Why don't you go to the bishop's house and speak to him? This is the truth- do not rush to go up to the bishop and tell him this, or an unimaginable torment will overtake you".

I answered him: "I had already prayed to you, lord, and I awaited your appearance for the third time, in order to announce without hindrance the revelation confirmed in this way".

As he stood and spoke to me, continuing to be in the same vision, I was thrilled and was transported to the city where I related all that I had seen to Bishop John.

In the same vision the bishop said to me: "If you, beloved, have had this vision, if what you are telling me has been truly revealed to you in our days, it is already on us that the rule of the law imposes the kindness to dig up this great plow-ox, the last of the line, which digs its deep furrow, and to hitch this vigorous ox likewise to the cart and to leave the field with the harvest which is coming."

"Lord," I said to him in the vision, "how can the field be left to me, if the plow-ox does not stay with me?" And he said to me, "This is how it should be, for this city pays tribute a great and heavy cart. This big cart needs a strong ox, which we want to get from you, that's why it is right to give this ox to this town, and the other two oxen with the young bulls will suffice for the work of plowing your field, for the great ox is helping".

And as soon as the bishop told me this, Gamaliel appeared to me, and he came to me, took my hand and led me to the field itself, saying: "If you want to find us, look for us in the field which is called in Aramaic 'Elaa-gabra', which translates to 'the men of God!".

As soon as I awoke after the third vision, I asked myself: "What is this field?" I told no one of this vision and alone I went to see this plowed land. It was a plain of great vistas, worthy of being proclaimed beautiful, and in the middle of this field was a sandy hill where I thought I had found the three bodies. I then returned to the city and I first informed the believers and the priests of merit so that they would teach me what I had to do.

They said to me: "Do you see what earthquakes, droughts, and kingdoms of rain are occurring one after the other every hour? You desire to cast your sight upon the clear vision which He reveals to the world through Christ for the love of mankind. Do not remain silent any longer".

First, the people went to Bishop John and spoke to him about me. He invited me to him, and asked me if it was really so.

"Truly, this is so" I insisted. And I related what had occurred to me- the first vision, the second, but as for the third I retained half of it, I told him nothing of what John had answered me concerning the ox, of whom I took the splint away from, the last in line, and I waited to hear him say that answer again. However, he raised his voice with great eagerness and said: "Blessed be the Lord! If you have really seen this, my beloved, it is because the Lord now desires to reveal his saints to us. It is therefore ordered that I take the bones of Saint Stephen, the first martyr and valiant archdeacon, a pious servant, who with his own eyes saw the celestial kingdom".

Then I told him the rest of the third vision, and he said to me: "Indeed, it is his real desire to discover these saints as they appeared to you in the vision".

He was filled with joy at this good news and he ordered me to go down to the village, to dig in that hill and look for them there.

"And when you find them, keep the place yourself and let me know by letter." Having received such an order from him, I went down to my village in the county all in the evening, saying to those around me: "Tomorrow, let us meet at dawn together to dig this very hill!"

The same night, Lord Gamaliel appeared to me and said to me: "Priest, do not tire yourself of digging in this hill, for this is not the place, this hill is only to bear witness to us. It is there on this hill that the ritual of mourning has been performed for our intention, but look for us north of the field. You will measure from the hill a distance of four hundred and seventy-four paces". Gamaliel appeared in the same way, the same night, to another monk, sincere and spotless, whose name was Megethe, and said to him: "Go tell Lucian priest. Do not tire yourself of looking for us on this hill, as we are not there, but in the north in the field".

And he showed him the place as well, where he had appeared to me. Then there appeared to me, Lucian, in the same place, three golden beds, two of them were lowered and on the third sat two men, one an old man and the other a young man. The beds were arranged so that one was raised and the other lowered, both were beautifully made.

And those who sat there in fine dress as those who are newly baptized. The third bed was adorned with a royal adornment woven with gold. At dawn as soon as we got up, we first took the direction of the hill. However, the monk held us back, saying: "Here is what was said to me in a vision to tell it to you". As soon as I heard, I understood that his vision was true. We had first taken the direction of the hill and after searching for three hours, we found a monument, on which was an inscription in Hebrew. We brought a scholar who knew Hebrew, and he read the inscription and said to me: "See what is written there. It is the place of lamentations and of righteousness".

So we left that place and went to the place we had seen on the night of the vision. We searched there all day and found exactly what had been revealed to us in the vision. On it was an inscription which was denoted thus in engraved relief: 'Qeleli ethnasuam', which translates as 'Geleliel', from the Aramaic, in Greek στέφανος, and from the Greek into the Georgian 'gwrgwn', meaning 'crown', and 'nasuam' meaning 'victorious in justice'. Gamaliel and Abiba, 'Gamaliel' meaning 'God conferred grace upon me', 'Abiba' means 'beloved son'. Immediately there was a great earthquake. The bones of Saint Stephen came alive and rejoiced. A very strong sweet odor came out of its chase and we all succumbed to light sleep as if intoxicated.

This sweet smell spread around and reached a distance of ten miles. From all four coasts, people came attracted by this sweet smell. I was told that all those who had been brought forth by this sweet odor found themselves, that day, cured of their infirmities and their illnesses.

I was then greeted by the holy bishop who came down, as well as two other bishops, and all accompanied by a large crowd. They rejoiced at the sight of the relics and solemnly carried Saint Stephen to Jerusalem with great honors and placed him in the sacred shrine. Gathered together, we built a dwelling worthy of the bones of Saint Stephen to glorify the Father, the Son, and the Holy Spirit, which befits His glory, power, and strength now and always in every age.

Amen.

II. — THE RETURN OF THE RELICS OF SAINT STEPHEN, ARCHDEACON AND FIRST MARTYR, FROM JERUSALEM TO CONSTANTINOPLE.

Prince Alexander had a martyr's crypt built, and asked Bishop John to bury the relics of Saint Stephen, the first martyr, there. The bishop then placed them in a reliquary on which he nailed a board. Saint Stephen, the first martyr, was very piously deposited there on December 15th, in the fifth indiction (between 407 and 417 AD), at the time of the consulship of our lord Constantine, during the autocratic reign of this same king.

At the end of five years, Alexander having fallen ill, made a will for the benefit of the Church and for the needy and, entrusting his family to God, he said: "If I die, make me a wooden reliquary and place me near the relics of Stephen, the first martyr. For it is I who, at my expense, have built his shrine." And having said this, he fell asleep.

Eight years after his death, his wife conceived the idea of taking the remains of her husband to her township, to Constantinople, and to accomplish this, she addressed Bishop Cyril of Jerusalem in these terms: "I want to bring the remains of my husband to my township, Constantinople. Can I let this happen?"
Bishop Cyril replied: "the people will move".
The wife then asked him, "Lord, will you give me my husband's relics?"
The bishop says in response only "no."

She then went home in tears and sent her father the letter written in these terms: "I, your beloved daughter, Julienne, greet you, being in desolation. I have made a beautiful and honorable offering. I beg you, be gracious for answering my prayer not as a request which is accomplished slowly, but as the word of the mystery of heaven addressed to my father. Being a widow, I am in danger, because the head of my family wants me to get married. Make haste, therefore, so that I may depart and bring with me the relics of my husband into my township, Constantinople. Hurry to get a letter from the king and send it to Bishop Cyril of Jerusalem.

Her father therefore obtained the order of the great king Constantine on January 15, of the Indiction of the same autocratic king, our lord.

It was the letter he sent her to Jerusalem and which she delivered to Bishop Cyril Jerusalem. Having seen and read it, the bishop did not know what to say. The woman came and said to him: "How can we do it, since we do not know which is the reliquary of Saint Stephen, the first martyr, and which is that of your husband? I don't know what we're going to do. Go and prepare for the journey, let me know and I will give you your husband's reliquary during the night."

So she got ready for the trip. She went to the Cathedral church, and at nightfall she went down to the chapel where the relics of Saint Stephen were deposited. When the door was opened, two reliquaries were found there. The bishop then said to the woman: "I do not know which is your husband's reliquary and which is that of Saint Stephen, the first martyr". However, she answered: "I know the reliquary of my husband, because it is I who made it". At these words the blessed bishop gave the order to take the reliquary which she was familiar with. She took off, kissed the relics of Saint Stephen, and took them off and put them on her mount. She took leave of the bishop and went away joyfully to pursue her own way.

Every night the angels sang during the journey, a sweet smell spread in the air and the evil spirits said aloud: "Woe to us! Where is Stephen going, the first martyr? He is coming to put us through the trial of fire." Meanwhile the woman was seated on her mount, and her slaves who walked those in front were dismayed and said: "What is it? The spirits call aloud to Saint Stephen. Could it be him without our knowing anything about it? For the multitude of angels walk before the reliquary and we are afraid. See, my lady, what are we going to do? Could it be that it is not the remains of your husband, but that we have the relics of Saint Stephen, the first martyr? What are we going to do, my lady?"

Having heard them, the noble lady began to cry and warned them: "Don't say anything about these terrible things that we have seen during this trip. If you are questioned in the villages or in the cities where we meet, say: "It is the reliquary of a noble that we are carrying to Constantinople".

Now, the same night we arrived at our station, the angels were silent during the day, but walked with us at the approach of evening and repeated aloud: "Gloria in excelsis Deo, in terra pax." For God revealed his angels to the slaves to protect them on the way. At midnight, the spirits said aloud: "Who is coming towards us? We do not have the strength to resist the holy relics, because they are of fire and they burn us by healing all those along the way armies of angels drove them out of the way so that they would not disturb Saint Stephen, the first martyr.

When we reached Ascalon on the shore of the sea, we found a ship ready to leave for Constantinople. The noblewoman invited the captain of the ship, gave him fifty drachmas and said to him, "I have a secret to tell you, do not object to me. I am taking a reliquary to Constantinople. Be rewarded by the Almighty."

Now, the boatman said: "Madam, get on the ship! I have nothing to reply to you, Madame, because the first martyr Stephen is great in your eyes and my hope is in him, because my eyes today have seen him glorified. Come, get on the ship so that it can leave, because we want to set out by the grace of God, with the help of the holy relic".

Hardly had we embarked when the ship, pushed by the wind, sailed away from the shore and soon found itself in the open sea. A huge wave shook and broke over its sails, and all the passengers were seized with terror. We got up and worshiped the holy relics. As we wept, fragrant air spread on the ship and the first martyr Stephen appeared and said to me: "Don't be afraid. I am near you". And with these words the wind subsided, there was a great calm and, in the evening, we crossed the abysses with a favorable wind.

At midnight, a great light occurred near the holy relics of the first martyr Stephen. We looked up and saw Our Lord Jesus Christ with the angels, who were singing: "Gloria in excelsis Deo, et in terra." For He was pleased with Saint Stephen who became a martyr in your name.

The Lord said to his angels: "Stay close to his holy relics, because he sacrificed his life in My name". And having said this, He rose towards heaven with the angels. When the day began to break, we arrived at the port and lowered the sails to grant the prerogative to the prince of the devils.

At the same time there was an earthquake so great that the foundations of the earth shook. It continued until the moment when the vessel of Saint Stephen, the first martyr, passed over it. It was then that the earthquake ceased. Now the demons cried and spoke to the prince: "Prince of the godless, why did you not burn the ship which has just passed near you? For you are the one who caused the earthquake. After having listened to them attentively, the prince did as they wished. He sent a force on purpose with the order to catch up and burn the ship. Yet, when the angels thought they were about to seize him, the angel engulfed them, to the great joy of all the passengers of the ship, for they felt that God was with them.

We sailed for three nights and three days before arriving at Chalcedon. The ship was brought into port, and we remained there for five days. All the tormented possessed of the devil who were on the coast, laughed while pronouncing these words: "The slave of the Lord has come, it is he whom the impious Jews have stoned. We must take it". Now, thanks to the holy relics of Saint Stephen, the first martyr, the spirits said: "Woe to us, he will burn us! Where shall we go to avoid this formidable being? And they came out of the men as those hunted by fire.

There, on the shore of Chalcedon, they brought infirm people as many as there were, because all were cured. And when leaving from there, we arrived at Souque, the whole town ran quickly to meet us, which did not fail to rejoice the Christians, while the pagans were displeased to hear it. From there we directed our boat towards the crowd passing on the other side of the shore. We came to Stavrion, a town called Zermon. Immediately, the blessed Archbishop Mitrophane sent to ask for the relics of Stephen, the first martyr. The whole multitude of pagans and Christians came running to see the power of the holy relics and then went to Emperor Constantine to inform him of the arrival of the relics of Stephen, the first martyr.

Now the Emperor asked them, "Tell me how the relics of Saint Stephen came here from Jerusalem? Who brought them forth? Then the noble woman was presented to him, saying to him: "Autocrat-Emperor, here is she who brought the relics of the saint and glorified Stephen, the first martyr."
The emperor then spoke to her: "Tell me the truth, how did you bring the relics of Stephen?"

This woman answered him: "Autocrat-Emperor, my blessed husband, Alexander, built the chapel of St. Stephen where, with the help of Bishop John, he buried his body. Several years later, my husband died leaving his will in the name of the bishop in which he formulated the following request: "If I die, place me near Saint Stephen, the first "martyr".

"And how did you bring the relics of Saint Stephen?" the emperor asked her. "Tell me the truth!"

Now she replied: "Autocrat-Emperor, being a widow, I suffered from the insistence of the prince who would force me to marry. So I informed my father of my desire to come here and bring my husband's relics to my township. It was then that my father received from your firmness the letter of authorization to withdraw the relics of my husband and sent it to Bishop Cyril and to me as well. We went down, Bishop Cyril and I, into the sepulcher and, instead of taking the remains of my husband, I took the relics of St. Stephen.

And the noble lady gave the letter to the king who read it and recognized its writing. The noble lady said to him: "Autocrat-Emperor, you have all power over my body, but God alone has all power over my soul. For it is God who works miracles in heaven and on earth.

My Lord, disturb me not. Send a Jew down to the ship, where the shrine of Saint Stephen, the first martyr is. On it a board is eluded there with an inscription in Hebrew. Let him read it and recognize its value". Now the Emperor Constantine called a Hebrew, made him take an oath, and said to him: "Look at what is written". The Hebrew left with two vice-consuls and, after having read the inscription, he said: "It is very admirable".

The vice-consuls, having asked what is admirable. The Hebrew answered them: "It is Stephen, the first martyr. Our salvation is from him, and my hope is in him, for my eyes today have seen him glorified." Then the vice-consuls departed and told the emperor that it was really Stephen, the first martyr. So the lord of the country rejoiced. He invited Mitrophane and he said: "Go, accompany the multitude, to the ship. I will send you a chariot to bring to the palace the reliquary of Stephen, the first martyr".

Then the patriarch walked towards the shore and all the people ran after him, carrying lighted candles. The patriarch Mitrophane then boarded the ship, removed the reliquary, which he placed on the chariot and hastened to return to the palace. The daughter of a boatman was on the bank at the same place, which is called Zeugama, because at this place the mules had harnessed the chariot on which were placed the relics of St. Stephen, the first martyr. This girl, possessed by the spirit of Python, cried out and said, "Oh! misfortune! Saint Stephen, first martyr, whence did he come to torment me? And the ungodly spirit knocked her down and came out of her without doing her any harm. This glorious miracle took place at the very place where the chariot, on which the shrine of Saint Stephen, was placed and was hitched up, but the mules refused to move forward. There was another woman suffering from a flow of blood. She had been bedridden for a long time in the same place which is called Stavrion. She had been very surprised to hear within her a voice saying to her: "Get up quickly and approach the chariot of Saint Stephen, the first martyr, who came among us from Jerusalem, before he sets out and does not return". She therefore hastened and came to Stavrion, where the shrine of St. Stephen, the first martyr, was and instantly the flow of blood ceased.

There was a sinful nobleman in Banto. His house was on the shore of Stavrion in the very place called Zeugama. He had a son of eighteen years of age, paralytic from birth. Having seen the miracles and healings that were being done, he hastened, took his paralytic son and arrived at the approaches to the coast of Stavrion, before the departure of the chariot and the reliquary of the first martyr Stephen. He threw his son, paralytic from birth, in front of the relics of St. Stephen the Martyr and, and the young man got up. He who was paralyzed, mounted the chariot and kissing the shrine of Stephen, the first martyr, shouted aloud: "Glory to you, Stephen, first martyr, you who have made the bonds that bedridden me". Having seen this glorious miracle take place and the healing that quickly followed, all the people unanimously glorified God.

However, the angels held back the mules of the chariot, who, having arrived at the place called Constantina, went no further. The mules could no longer advance and retreated back. One of them spoke, thanks to the angel, with a human tongue and, addressing the people, said: "Why do you beat me in the face? You must put that down. Do not wear it anywhere else. Otherwise, you will see miracles and other wonders".

The bishop, being very alarmed, and not wanting to torment the animals, sent word to the emperor, saying: "It is impossible for us to bring the relics of Saint Stephen". At this the king was very unhappy to hear the news and sent about fifteen other mules to drag the chariot. They tried until they were weary, but their efforts were in vain, because the angels held back the chariot.

Then, the whole people raised their voices: "The Almighty God stands alone, he alone works miracles because of the first martyr, holy among the saints, the one who was martyred in the name of God. Lord, grant us thanksgiving, through the prayer and the intercession of your first martyr Stephen.

It was then that the bishop took the reliquary from the chariot and placed it on the ground. There, for several months, he built a church and they stayed with the relics observing great piety. Blessed Mitrophane, Patriarch of

Constantinople, placed them in the church in August. The healings of the sick and the wonders were done during all that time, and the people remained with Saint Stephen, the first martyr. Mitrophane the patriarch said, addressing the people: "Listen and understand, you who remain with Saint Stephen, the first martyr! Treat martyrdom with zeal every hour! Martyrs provoke words of praise and urge these words to be uttered. They obtained grace and they shine even after their death. Buried in their sepulcher, they plead for our justification, and give thanks to His Hand. They are seated as on the throne of God, because the souls of the just are in the Hands of God. Torments will never touch them. Here is how Luke revealed, in the eulogy of Stephen, the first martyr, the graces obtained by him, because he said: "Stephen was filled with the Holy Spirit and the strength of God. He did great miracles and wonders among the people and the grace of God was in him". Stephen, filled with the strength and grace of God, was perfectly plenitude, and filled with prudence. Stephen was a treasury full of the blessings of the most Holy Spirit. Through him were accomplished very great works. In this world he granted health to the legs of the lame. He restored sight to the blind. He drove out diseases from the infirm. He expelled demons, and he reconnected the detached nerves of the paralytics. He lavished his care on widows and was the father of orphans. For he spoke marvelous words and did great signs and wonders among the people. That's not all. He showed his love for the Jews themselves, he preached Christ to them, and always, Stephen, the first martyr, the one who had become worthy to see the Lord, said to them three things: "O impious Jews, why have you dishonored and insulted the One who glorified you, Our Lord Jesus Christ. Ungodly Jews, you hanged Him who raised you. You have crucified Him, the One to whom you owe your salvation. You have rejected your Savior".

And Saint Stephen then said to them: "He confirmed the testament made to Abraham, to the generation of Leah, and the oath made to Isaac. He confirmed his order to Jacob and the eternal testament to Israel. He gave you the land of Canaan. It is He who overthrew Egypt for you with the death of the first-born. O impious Jews, it is He who split the Red Sea and made you cross it as on dry land. It is He who swallows up Pharaoh and his people in the Red Sea. It is He who enlightened your way every night with a pillar of fire and covered you every day with clouds. It is He who gave you as leaders Moses and Aaron going before you. It is He who made you pious in Horeb, gave you manna in the desert and made you drink water from the rock. It is He who has destroyed mighty kings for you, Siho, king of the Amorites, Hog, king of Bashan. It is He who for you, O impious Jews, has bound seven tribes and destroyed their kings and given you their land to dwell in. It is He who has destroyed cities for you, overthrown ramparts, demolished towers and given you, you impious Jews, a land to settle there. It is He who brought you from Egypt and transplanted you like a veritable fertile vine. He has stretched out your horns to the sea, your treetops to the rivers. O vineyards of truth, why have you become bitter and have produced no grapes? But you have erred, and lied in impiety, and you cry, 'Seize him and crucify him.'

O impious Jews, you had only bad intentions for him who healed your sick, as our Lord Jesus Christ did, and purified your lepers. He restored health to your sick, as the Lord Jesus Christ did, and you, impious people, have prepared the cross for him. He healed your paralytics, as Lord Jesus Christ healed them, and you thought of having him put to the gallows. He raised your dead, as the Lord Jesus Christ did, and you have prepared death for him, you O impious Jews".

Now, Saint Stephen was interested in them: "Lord, do not punish them for the evil they have done. O ungrateful Jews, you have by your acts relieved the benefactor God who sees you taken out of Egypt, leading you by the firm hand and by the high arm. Arriving at the edge of the sea, you did not glorify him for his miracles, on the contrary you said: 'Are our graves not in Egypt from where he dragged us to exterminate us?' He gave you manna in the desert and your heart wanted to eat garlic. He filled you with honey and your heart wanted to drink gall. You murmured against Moses and you irritated Aaron's spirit. You turned away from the beginningless God and demanded that you be allowed to return to Egypt. Moses intended to go up on the mountain and to bring the law written by the fingers of God. During this time, you made a golden calf at Horeb and you prostrated yourself before the sculpted figure and you offered the sacrifice to this same idol.

So to punish you he became angry, he scattered you among the pagans, he took you there and you mingled with the pagans, you learned their customs and you worshiped the star of our God Jesus Christ. How shall I glorify you and praise you? And how can I say praise worthy of you about Your deeds?" So I can't watch the image of Saint Stephen the First, martyr, as I said before.

Oh! His image is like that of the Lord and his shining face is like the sun. And just as it is impossible to look the sun in the face, I cannot look at the face of Saint Stephen, the first martyr". It is he who prays to the great Lord to give paradise to the world. Stephen, you who disdained the stones and rejoiced in heaven with the angels, you whom the waves did not swallow up, you who were not afraid of the stones and the fire did not burn, you who walked on earth, acted as a citizen of heaven and, numbered among the angels, were standing before the Lord Jesus Christ, open your eyes, because you shine on earth with a splendor that is more brilliant than that of the stars or that of the sun, defend your fellow citizens, you, Stephen the first martyr.

Do not let ill-intentioned demons seduce men but drive them out by the strength of your holy relics. By God fiery Stephen saw the heavens opened and the Lord of the Sabbath seated on the throne of cherubs, and the Son of man seated at the right hand of powers. This is why Stephen rushed to the Lord Jesus Christ to acquire the crown braided with pearls of many colors. The saints aspired to this crown of the just. It is for her that they have become the militant knights of the great Lord, because of this I pray to you God-Christ to grant peace to the world through His intercession, to appease the struggles, to help the sailors, to satisfy the fishermen, and to fill the earth with fruits of the soil.

When coming forth, Stephen shone in the world by the grace of the majestic holy Christ, of the great splendor of our Lord and God. The emperor Constantine glorified God in Constantinople and the whole city rejoiced at the sight of the holy relics of Stephen, the first martyr. For the Emperor Constantine had, thanks to God, the grace of Jesus Christ. Now, Stephen deserved the grace of heaven and an imperishable coronet. He granted healing to men, harbor to boatmen, and fish to unfortunate fishermen. Lord, heal the sick, deliver the possessed, grant sight to the blind, restore the paralytic, be merciful to widows, raise orphans.

Crown him who is martyred for the faith, O Lord, for you are great and terrible to all your peoples, and all those that pray to you. Lord, do not count their pockets. Beware, my brothers, of dishonoring him. Let us observe the commandments of Our Lord Jesus Christ. He who saved us from darkness and called us into the kingdom of heaven, for to Him belongs the strength of the Father, that of the Son and that of the Holy Spirit now, every day and throughout the ages. Amen.

IV. — SPEECH OF GREGORY, PRIEST OF ANTIOCHE, ON STEPHEN THE FIRST MARTYR.

We have a good memory in front of us, my beloved ones, a reason to write to the Churches of Christ on the acts of Saint Stephen, the first martyr. He accomplished for us, his intercession for the soul, his retort, his acceptance of torments, his death, his coronation and three times the revelation of martyrdom. At that time, after the Incarnation of Our Lord Jesus Christ and two years after the passion on the cross, His death, resurrection and ascension, when He returned to his Father, a certifying inquiry was made among the Jews, among the Sadducees and Pharisees, and among the pagans concerning Jesus Christ of Nazareth. They sought how He was born, He, the firstborn, how He was raised, how He was crucified, being incarnate, and how he died and rose from the dead. Some said that it is the prophet who appeared, others said: "No, on the contrary, he deceived the world". But still others said, "He is truly the son of God." And great trouble ensued among the people, so that the doctors and philosophers of Ethiopia, Thebaid, Alexandria, Jerusalem, Asia, Mauritania and Babylonia all came together. From the first hour until the fourth the trouble was as great as tremendous thunder.

Then Stephen, a man of letters and a philosopher, beloved of all the people, from the tribe of Abraham and from the family of Benjamin, rose to a height, stretched out his hand and pronounced aloud: "My brothers, young and old, listen to what I have to answer you. Why do your cries rise more and more and why does all Jerusalem come together? Blessed be the man who does not doubt Jesus Christ, Son of the living and invisible God, He who is charity in person by his nature. He descended from heaven, because of the sins and ignorance of the people, into the bosom of the Blessed Virgin, chosen from the beginning of the world. As Adam, the father of the world, called his wife and said: 'Be called the mother and the life!', likewise she was named Virgin and lived according to the Scriptures. She agreed to it being so. Christ was born as a man by likeness, without emptiness. When he was born as a man, the whole earth was enlightened. However, the enemy was watching. When he had taken a body and was still a young child, Herod became worried and resolved to exterminate the newborns of that time. Three thousand were killed by him. Now, this happened for the love of mankind, so that the holy children might intercede for the salvation of men, and make the blind see and heal your lepers. He drove out the demons from you in the same way of that first seduction, that of the tree, which disappeared from you. He planted a venerable tree. He is believed to have descended into hell for all, he destroyed him who had the power of death. He rose again on the third day and gave life to all. Woe to the infidels on the day he comes a second time to judge the living and the dead. Fire will precede Him and a great storm will break out." He had not yet finished his sermon when the whole multitude of the people cried out: "Take him off the face of the earth, take Stephen away!" For he has pronounced an outrageous speech on this chosen holy place.

They seized him and led him to Pilate, crying, "Remove him from the face of the earth!" And Pilate exclaimed aloud and said, "Besides speaking to you of the holy and righteous son of God, I do not see that this man is wicked. It would be a blessing if I were not compelled by you to lay my hand on the imperishable and just lord. Why are you mad and why are you gnashing your teeth at Stephen? You see that his face is similar to that of an angel. Be less angry and do not be in vain against this man!"

Then, all advanced in the middle of the assembly talking and arguing: "What shall we do with this man?" Now Caiaphas, the high priest, ordered him to be beaten with clubs and guarded. Yet, the saint rejoiced. The next day he was taken with Saul of Tarsus, from Caesarea in Palestine, in order to reach Jerusalem more quickly.

For it was Saul who had received the authority, and it was to him that the high priests were to present with bound feet those who confessed the faith of Christ. As soon as he saw the letters of the high priest of the assembly, he quickly returned to Jerusalem. He threatened Stephen and gnashed his teeth. However, the following day, he sat down on the steps of the Temple and ordered to present this champion of Christ and he said to him: "I admire the beauty of your face and your proven wisdom. How did you commit the error of announcing that the crucified is God? You have troubled all the people in their religion. I have traveled around the city, the cities of Judea and the villages of Damascus and Galilee. Your wisdom replaced me in my affairs, and I am surprised that you too have obliged me to return to this city. I, who found myself in a distant country, having come so far. Because of this, I beg your teaching and your learned mind to observe the religion transmitted by your elders. Do not divert the people from their ways and do not gather them all around you. For what advantage will follow, if you disturb your desires, you will become angry. My intention is to inflict a chastisement upon you, you such as you are, image of the angel, you who are related to me bodily."

Then the blessed Stephen, stretching out his hands and addressing him, said to him the following words: "Be calm, Saul, persecutor of the churches of Christ! Calm your violence, enraged against the flock. Do not defile our race, away from the living God. Denying the son of God, your hope of the salvation of the world, understand that we are both of the same lineage. We are the offspring of glorious Abraham, of Jacob, of the house of Benjamin. For I spare your nobility, and I tell you what I see in advance, that in a few days you will have to drink this potion. Do, therefore, quickly what you are going to do, because I am ready to die in the name of the son of the Supreme God".

Then Saul, irritated, tore his clothes with own hands and beat Stephen with a stick. Now Gamaliel, the Doctor of Religion, who had taught Saul, rose up and struck him on the cheek, and said to him: "Did you learn such a doctrine from me, O Saul? By insulting those who have become worthy of grace and resembling the divine image of Christ? Or do you not know that we are born of Him and that it is He that we have acquired our deeds. Do you hear how everything that has been said to you by him is pleasing to God and to men!"

Yet, Saul became more and more irritated, and with a changed face, addressed Gamaliel: "I pity your wisdom and I respect what you have taught me. If you do the same thing again, even once, you will have to answer with words of art for your ardor".

Gamaliel said, "Will I be blessed if I become worthy to suffer for my Christ!" Then, all uttered the chant: "Let them be crucified who utter words of outrage." So Saul and the chief priests tried to keep Stephen until the next day. In the meantime, the blessed prayed and said: "Lord, do not count this sin against them!

Now the angel of the Lord came down from heaven strengthening him. Then the numerous multitude of the people believed in God and the whole of the church of Christ increased because of Stephen, because he was a prophet and master of all things. The next day all the tribes of the people held a meeting and led him out of the city to punish him.

Now the saint climbed on a rock near the holy Mount of Olives, lifted up his voice and said to them, "How long will the devil blind your hearts and prevent you from discerning the light and truth? For behold, the law and the prophets first prepared the ways of the Lord, and they announced the birth of Christ as a man. First, Deuteronomy says, 'When the time comes, I will send my Word by the spirit of childbirth through the innocent way of the Immaculate Virgin, and the fruit of righteousness will grow on uncultivated and unsown ground".

And Isaiah said, 'Behold, the Virgin shall conceive. She will father a son and we will call him Emmanuel. And again: 'A boy was born to us- the son is granted to us.' And the prophet Nathan said: 'I saw a virgin having no knowledge of a husband, a child in her arms, and all was enlightened, and the prince of this world will flee to the ends of the universe'. What's the use of talking a lot? You have closed your eyes so as not to see, and you have been deaf so as not to hear the words of the Supreme God. Was it not your fathers who pursued some prophets who foretold the coming of the Righteous and did they not kill them?" Having said this, he looked up to heaven and he saw the glory of God, Jesus standing at the right side of God, as it was said 'Behold, I see the heavens opened, and the Son of Man standing at the right hand of God.'

They squealed loudly and put their hands over their ears. He said to them, "Do not say, His blood be on us and on our children. I fear that the wrath of the Lord will overtake you and your children, as you have said". They raised their voices all at the same time and said: "Cut him down with stones!" The executioners looked at each other, yet none dared not touch him, because he was the most glorious among the people. Saul flew into a rage, took the executioners' clothes, put them in a place and immediately they laid hands on Stephen. The first martyr Stephen looked at Saul and said to him: "Saul, what you have done to me will be done to you justly by these very Jews, so that you will suffer and remember me."

So, they hit him harder and harder, throwing stones. Their great number prevented the sun's rays from being seen. Now, Stephen bent his knees and sayid, "Jesus Christ, receive my soul and do not take into account this sin they have committed against you and against me, your servant." Thereafter, he fell asleep.

There was then much weeping and lamentation and the believers were persecuted. Now, Gamaliel, got up in the night, and asked the apostles to take the relics of the saint and bring them to his village. He accomplished the quarantine in accordance with the rules of their law. The needs of the mourners were met at the expense of Gamaliel. So he put him in a new tomb which was unfinished and was about forty miles from the city. At the announcement of this event, Nicodemus, nephew of Gamaliel, who had learned during the night from Jesus the Savior, of rebirth by water and by the spirit, so he went away and received baptism from the hands of Peter and John, pupils of the Lord.

After hearing him, the high priests and the Pharisees became angry with him and intended to kill him like the first martyr Stephen. Yet, they did not do the same thing to Gamaliel, they excommunicated him, carried away into the house of their temple, and all that belonged to him drove him out of the city, covered him with wounds, tormented him, and abandoned him. Now, Gamaliel was collected in the same village where Lucian had exercised his priesthood. He fed him at his own expense and clothed him until the time when Gamaliel also died a few days later. Everything was accomplished as for a confessor of Christ and Lucian buried him near Saint Stephen.

The fourth man who is buried near them, his name is Abibos. He was his beloved son, he was twenty years old. He studied the law more than his father did, then he learned the scriptures of God, like his father, he believed in the predictions of God and with him he received the same day from the same apostles the baptism at the baptismal font. Stephen, first martyr of Christ, died on December 27th to glorify the Father and the Son and the Holy Spirit present and always in all age. Amen.

V. — THE OPENING OF SAINT GREGORY THE PRIEST: PRAISE OF STEPHEN. FIRST MARTYR.

My brothers, I consider today's feast as a dazzling day for you, because I have remembered the deeds of Stephen, the first martyr. Direct your thoughts to me, as I pray for you. Bow down silently as under the weight of my poor words, so that you may benefit. For such is the beginning of the teaching of the martyr. Luke says in the Acts of the Apostles: "Stephen was full of faith and by the Holy Spirit did the greatest miracles and wonders." Stephen the famous martyr, Stephen the cluster of good fruits, Stephen of the beautiful crown, Stephen desiring the crown of heaven, Stephen who fought for the crown, Stephen this joy of the saints, Stephen who shows the way for every fighter to reach the imperishable crown, Stephen the beginning of the martyrs, the one who had the hope that the crown is ready for him in heaven. He was standing in the midst of the scribes and the Pharisees, he unveiled their impieties and said to them: 'You always rise up against the Holy Spirit, like your fathers.'

Oh! The audacity of the true and the just! Oh! The wrath of the impious assembly! Stephen remained standing and presented them with righteousness. He taught them like brothers, but they hardly acquiesced in what he had told them. They gritted their teeth, like the wild beasts that leap on the lamb. They would kill the righteous, because they could not stand his accusation. Now, Christ has woven the celestial crown for Stephen. Why, Jews do you imitate God in this way? Stephen, speaks of God, but you run to kill him. He therefore runs to heaven. You rush to get him away from this life, albeit temporary, but he has the sweetness of eternal life. You chased him away of the city, but he, thanks to you, he became one of the celestial powers and was a judge worthy of the ineffable and moving vision, this is why he did not pass over in silence what he had seen, but he thundered against the Jews. He bridled them. You are the impious Jew, but he is a Christian, the holy fruit of Christ. You associate yourself with the Pharisees, but he participates in the goods of the Holy Trinity, he is his heir. You have the law and you do not observe it, but he has Christ, the son of God, and preaches him. You killed the prophets as enemies, but he received grace and the Holy Spirit and he drove out the infirmities of our race in the name of Christ.

Why are you getting carried away? Why do you crave the healing of the sick? Why do you envy the miracles done by us? Why do you tend to his death more than to his eternal life? Certainly, because the greatest profit comes from the enemies, since all the martyrs and the righteous, fought by the enemies and those who tolerated, were crowned.

If the enemies did not fight, they would not have won their victory. If they had not inaugurated the lists, they would not have had to fight. If they had not killed them, as they had unto the Lord, they would not have been crowned. It suffices, O Jews, to have studied the Lord, having erected for Him the cross and having nailed to it the one who was the image of man because of Adam. Now you suddenly take up arms against His warrior. You cannot resist the wisdom and the spirit of what he says, because, O Jews, you really cannot oppose Christ in whose name He deliberates, because it is hard for you to rush beating the rock with the spur, the rock which is Christ.

Leave him, O envious Jew, a few days respite, so that the lame, injured and sick of your people may be healed, let him work miracles, so that he, helping many, may surrender to the Lord your God, and know His true Son, first born of the brother as a divinity before the ages and lastly incarnated in the bosom of the Virgin. It was for us He became man. Although you have wanted to hold back Our Lord Jesus Christ so that he ceases to perform miracles, it is precisely now that more than before the performance of miracles by his disciples is taking place.

For the Lord said: "He who believes in Me will also do what I do and he will do more". You saw proof and marveled at the healing of the lame man, and you roared around him like a lion. As to the Apostles of Christ, Peter and John, you saw that the people brought them possessed by ungodly spirits and sick people who had been healed.

What have you to say, O Jews without exploits? You see the business of God and you hardly glorify God, on the contrary, you get angry and you make death threats.

O wisdom of the Jews struggling against God! O wrath of the Pharisees! O wisdom of impious priests! O unconsciousness of the unreasonable! O vain thoughts of the irreligious! O their hard and so shrewd spirit! O their deviant and vicious conscience. O blessed and thrice praised Stephen, say what suits them. O you, pleasing to God, to Christ and to the Holy Spirit, speak of their irreligion. O most holy Stephen, venerable in the camp of the believers, speak what is proper to them. O chosen of God and fellow citizen of Christ, tell the irreligious Jews fighting against God what the Holy Spirit taught you to say. For the Lord says to his disciples: "When you are brought to a meeting, do not worry about what you say, for the Holy Spirit will teach you in due time what to say".

Now Stephen looked with sadness at the blindness of their hearts and was wounded by the spiritual ardor of God. He spoke these words to them: "Do you still revolt against the Holy Spirit, like your fathers? You have always shown ingratitude towards God, like your fathers. You have become perpetual enemies of the saints and murderers of the prophets, like your fathers, and now you complete the measure of your fathers, as my Lord says."

"And I imitate my Lord, O Jews, and I do not fear to die in his name, for I live by him always; it is He who gives life to all, it is He who created the heavens and founded the earth."

"It is He who said to Abraham: 'Come out of the land, from the tribe and from the house of your father, and come to the land which I will show you.' He gave him the sign of the circumcision. He fathered Isaac. It was he who blessed Isaae and delivered Jacob from the wrath of his brother Esau. It was He who gave Joseph grace in the eyes of Pharaoh of the Egyptians."

"It is He who multiplied our nation in Egypt, who delivered our fathers from their captivity, who led them into the desert and overwhelmed Pharaoh and his chariots in the Red Sea. It is He who, through Moses, gave grace and the law to our fathers. He said to them by his mouth, 'The Lord will make you a prophet, like me and you, and more To your brothers'. He was therefore speaking of Christ: 'However, you read well every day that you are blind, it is your heart that sees nothing'."

Hearing this, they looked for ways to kill him. They looked at him in anger, but they saw his face like an angel and were amazed. For Stephen was filled with the Holy Spirit. He looked towards heaven and, having seen the glory of God and Christ standing at the right hand of God, he said: "Behold, I see the heavens opened and the son of man standing at the right hand of God!"

And with these words, the wicked stopped their ears with their hands, suddenly threw themselves on him like Zealots of the law and began to stone this just man. And he was praying saying, "Lord, take my soul! He bent his knees, uttered a prayer and said, "Lord Jesus Christ, don't count that among their sins".

O peaceful nature of the just! O magnanimity of the brave knight! O blameless soul of the worthy! What are you to say, Stephen? You tolerate being beaten with stones, you endure the harshness of malice and you pray for them! Come and look at this second Moses, hero, this second David at the same time and again this second Samuel!

For Moses said: "Lord, if you forgive them their sins, forgive well, if not, also free me from this book, in which you inserted me!" David said, "Lord, cast your wrath on me and on my father's house, but not on your people!" Samuel said, "Let it not be because of me that you disdain my prayer to God for them!" Like them, Stephen said: "Lord Jesus Christ, let this pöch& be of no account to them." And that's how he spoke, he, knocked down under the stones and put to death. He did not become like the Jews who fight against God.

Although having been one of them, he turned out to be their superior. He was Jewish by birth, but he became a Christian and accepted the Holy Spirit. He was an apostle and confessor of Christ our God. He received the incorruptible crown in heaven and, associated with the holy angels, he is our general intercessor in the paradise of Jesus Christ Our Lord, to whom belongs glory with his Father and the gracious and vivifying Holy Spirit, present and always and from century to century. Amen.

VI. — PRAISE OF SAINT STEPHEN, FIRST DEACON AND FIRST CONFESSOR,

O beloved, it is the graces and the talents that the Holy Spirit had distributed that the new Church presented today to her fiance, the immortal king. And, like the heavens, theirs fresh from the new paradise, not from the first paradise which remained uncultivated through disobedience, but from that which was cultivated by the docile preachers of the Gospel of Christ and grew magnificently and became fruitful.

For the grain of pure wheat did not fall to the earth in vain, it did not die in vain, but as he had said it died to produce more fruit.

He gave to his Church, to keep as a treasure, the first the apostle confessors, these fragrant flowers. In the second place their works, the good fruits of their acts in which the Church always finds her delight and her rejoicing. Beloved, today the apostles gain power and the confessors appear. Today the prophets become examples, and the martyrs triumphant. Today the Lord reveals his cross and the choice fighters appear. Today the new foundation of the churches is established and the fighters of Christ discover their beauty in the vaults of the churches like the firm stones hewn out of the rock of Christ. Today the prophecy of David and that of Isaiah are fulfilled, for around Jerusalem new walls are erected, whose stones are precious stones, sapphires. These are the holy apostles and martyrs.

For the walls of the ancient law have crumbled and the churches of new grace, the gospel of Christ, surround Jerusalem as with a wall. Today the believers are multiplying and the assembly of the apostles is crowned. Today the preachers of the gospel of Christ are growing strong and the servants of the old law are weakening. The lost lambs of the house of Israel which had fled from the court of their Lord, having fallen prey to wild beasts of their own volition, dwindled in number, and the wild flocks of the heathen filled a court inaccessible to beasts. The sons of the law-giving prophets become the debtors of God, the obstinate, hard-hearted, and circumcised and uncircumcised, rise up against the Holy Spirit as adversaries in heart and soul. The poor in spirit shine, bowing their heads and receiving the light of baptism by water and by the spirit. Today, Christ has placed on the heads of the churches the crowns of the apostles, those of famous events.

Stephen is indeed the crown according to his name, the grace of beauty in the hands of the Lord.

Stephen, one of the assembly of the apostles, one of the seventy, who advances at the head of the seven deacons, is the champion among the pupils of Christ, the greatest of confessors, prince of martyrs, leader of the combatants, precursor of struggle on the list of the valiant and carrying the price of the most prompt victory, deacon of the earth and knight of the sky, angel of this world and man in the highest of the heavens.

Stephen the Handsome, with works surpassing his name, deacon by modesty and holiness, preacher of Christ by faith, apostle by choice, prince of the knights of Christ, commander of the army of the great King and servant of the celestial altar. Who is worthy of glory in such a high degree, as you are, you, the most praised amongst the martyrs and the most distinguished among the deacons? We can't find anyone like you.

O blessed Stephen, who of human beings first appeared in the image of an angel and immediately succeeded in taking his place at the front of the battle. Chief of the deacons and chief among the martyrs, O thou, the first crowned among the angels, glorified on earth and honored in heaven. He saw with his own eyes the immutable celestial heritage prepared by Christ and he inherited it instantly.

It was therefore commanded that the holy and blameless servant of the well-known altar should advance in a splendid manner to the spiritual sanctuary of the heavenly altar above as the spiritual servant of the [...] spiritual [...]. Thus were to be fulfilled the words of the Saviour: "Where I am, there also will be my servant". O you, brilliant in body and brilliant in spirit, how did you come so quickly to the divine table above the vaults of the earth, where you do not share the body and blood of the Son of God, but through your intercession favors and graces are distributed to those who love God with all their soul through the living and supplicating Christ, who has worthily crowned you!

Before the impious Jews crushed you with stones, Jesus Christ hastened to show you his reign with the Father in the highest heaven. Moses and the other prophets were not worthy to see God appear to them on earth with their own eyes, and he, Moses, unable to see the terrible God and His glory, that fire, hid himself in the cleft of the mountain.

But you, image of the angels of light, you have split so much air from earth to heaven and you have broken the strength of the winds. Rows of stars and thick clouds fled before your eyes. You have split the heights of the heavens and the waters of the upper heavens. You have passed near the authorities and the powers, the armies of heaven. You saw there, O Stephen nature itself, ineffable essence, incomprehensible power, dreadful and marvelous existence of the Father and of the Son and of the Holy Spirit. You said and testified to the unbelievers: "Behold, I see the heavens opened and the Son of man at the right hand of God".

It is because of this that you were stoned. you, blessed deacon of the true God and preacher of Christ your God. Who would be able to praise you, you, prince of the leaders of the army, valiant and distinguished? If all tongues met, they would not even be able to praise you worthily, you, Stephen, crown, model of the angels and with them of Christ. How will your eyes, shining by the grace of God, bear the dreadful flame, the matter of fire, the blaze of the sun?

For the bright light of the sun dazzles your eyes. On the contrary, you saw the king of heaven, as in a mirror. Your impious murderers were thinking of tearing you from this earth and they did not know that they had led you, you stoned, to heaven near the crucified. You, whom they expelled from Jerusalem to deprive you of all shelter, you are a citizen of heavenly Jerusalem to the assembly of myriads of angels, this is what they themselves have revealed. Not that you failed to be numbered among the apostles, but you became the degree by which the first apostles ascended to heaven and you opened the way for all the martyrs who follow you to go to heaven which is the royal abode in heaven.

You are the one who, ahead of all the apostles, fulfills the orders of the Lord who says: "Whoever wants to follow me and come to me, let him renounce himself, let him carry his cross and come follow me." Since you did not remain the same after the crucifixion, the resurrection and the ascension, in heaven and the ardor of your love for Him and your desire drew you towards Him, towards Gelui who had filled you with his

grace before your martyrdom, O blessed!

Who does not celebrate Christ who crowned you? Who does not envy your holiness, humility and modesty, those virtues which are proper to you? You who have become so like Him, to forgive them and absolve their irrational conduct. O blessed Stephen, true archdeacon, irreproachable dove, who by your race was sacrificed for the sake of the crucified Christ. You the real dove of Zion which is always domiciled there, it is the habit of the dove to sojourn in foreign residences or with other birds.

In the same way you, blessed, you hastened by the span of your wings and by your soul in heaven, before the God who introduced you into the house of his Father where there are many dwellings. (As for your holy body, you did not want it to remain in foreign dwellings, nor in the midst of foreign companions, but you returned it to Zion, beautiful apostolic temple of God, whose door is pleasant to the Lord more than all the dwellings of Jacob are.

It is there that the ardent zeal to seek your holy relics receives healing and the grace of Christ the Lord, who has crowned you with glory and honors. You have astonished the hosts of heavenly angels. Seeing that you are similar to their image ascending with your soul near the Lord, they came to meet you and welcomed you into their honorable abode.

From your martyrdom Saul rejoices, as it was as Paul, persecutor of Christ, he who held the churches in captivity, who was once your master in the mosaic law. Moreover, it is he who stands with your murderers and shares in your martyrdom. However, Saul did not know that he was sending you beforehand to Christ as his intercessor. This is why he completed the number of your martyrdom during your short-term mission and became a preacher of the divinity of Christ. He fought for the Churches and directed them. He manifested himself as an imitator of your martyrdom and a pangyrist of your fellow men, preaching the gospel of Our Lord Jesus Christ.

O you, glory of those who are glorified in Christ, crown of the churches for Christ, helper of those who struggle, master of the Orthodox, invincible by wisdom, full of the grace of the Holy Spirit, it is because of your coronation that the apostles are glorified, that the martyrs rejoice, the believers rejoice, the combatants multiply and the prophets see their prophecies fulfilled by you. The Church is enlightened by your holy relics and day by day you have become the foundation of martyrs, and we, priests, deacons and all the people believing in Christ, we celebrate your memory and have recourse to your love of holiness.

Pray, Stephen, Christ our God that we keep your invincible faith and be delivered from all the temptations of this world and that the innocent come before the throne of Jesus Christ our Lord, who with His Father and the Holy Spirit befit glory and honors now and always and from century to century, Amen.

VII. — THE 28TH OF THE MONTH OF DECEMBER, COMMEMORATION OF SAINT PETER THE APOSTLE AND THE MARTYRDOM OF PETER IN ROME EIGHT DAYS BEFORE THE FESTIVAL OF ROSE.

The Blessed Peter rejoiced with God in Rome with his brothers and gave thanks to God day and night that the believing people had come in the name of our Lord Jesus Christ. King Agrippa's concubines also frequented Saint Peter to hear and learn the word of God. The names of these women were: Agrippina, Icaria, Euphemie, and Doris. As soon as they had heard from Peter the holy words of Christ, their hearts suddenly returned to the service of God and they agreed to stay out of the defilement of Agrippa's bed, whose abuses made them suffer much.

However, as they did not submit, Agrippa was worried and afflicted all the more because he loved them passionately. He appointed spies and gave them the mission to find out where they were going. They then told him that they were going to Peter. Having called for them, he said to them: "This Christian has taught you not to have relations with me. Know then that I will destroy you and that I will burn him". Now they preferred to bear all the torments on the part of Agrippa rather than suffer from any defilement and they became strong by the power of Christ.

However, there was another well-made woman, wife of Alphian, friend of the emperor, who was called Xanthippe. When she saw many other women with Peter, she too separated from her husband Alphian. And Alphian was amazed at Xanthippe's treacherous love for him, for she would not even go to bed with him. Alphian, furious like a wild beast, wanted to tear Peter apart with his own hands. He understood very well that it was because of Peter that his wife had separated from him. Other noble matrons, likewise moved by the holy words they heard from St. Peter, also separated from their husbands. Wives moved away from their husbands' beds, wanting to persevere their holiness and live their lives piously.

Then Rome was alarmed and Alphian also informed Agrippa of his affair. He went to find him and said to him: "Avenge the injury that this man has caused me, by separating my wife from me, otherwise I will avenge myself".

Agrippa replied, "I am afflicted with the same disease from that man, O Alphian."

"Why do you neglect this case, O Agrippa"? resumed Alphian. "Let us therefore seize him as a malefactor and kill him, so that our wives stay with us and we become the avengers of those who are not in a condition to avenge themselves and whose wives have also been separated. by this man.

While they were thus deliberating, having heard the advice given by her husband Agrippa, Xanthippe sent a warning to Peter to come out of Rome. At the same time other brothers with Marcel begged him to leave the city of Rome. Now Peter said, "Should I flee now? Never. It will not be".

"No, no," they said, "that's not it. You are still able to serve God". He therefore submitted to their word and left the city of Rome alone, saying to them: "Let none of you go out with me."

And Peter said, "I will go out alone changing the shape of my clothing". And as Peter passed through the gate of the city of Rome, he saw the Lord Himself enter into the city. As soon as he saw the Lord, Peter said to him, "Where are you going, Lord?" The Lord answered him: "I am entering the city of Rome to be crucified". Peter then answered saying: "Are you going, my Lord, have you crucified again?" Returning to himself, Peter saw the Lord ascend to heaven and he immediately returned to Rome. He rejoiced and glorified God, because he had seen the Lord and had asked him: "Lord, are you going to be crucified a second time?"

He went up to his brothers and told them everything he had seen and heard. Now, the brothers were disheartened and worried in their hearts. They wept and said: "We beg you, our Lord Peter, to take care of us who are a young nursery."

And Peter said to them: "Since it is the will of the Lord, the Lord is able, even if we take no care of you, to strengthen you in His faith and to establish you on the foundation, plantation which He himself had made. And you yourselves edify one another, allied on the same basis. For by the will of the Lord I remained with you bodily and did not neglect my duties. Now, by his will, I go away rejoicing and cheerful, my Lord".

While Peter was saying these words and his brothers wept in despair, four executioners came, seized St. Peter and led him to Agrippa because of his displeasure. However, Agrippa imputed to Peter a great offense and he ordered him to be crucified. A large gathering of brothers, rich and poor, formed. They were orphans and widowers, men and women, and they wanted to see St. Peter and to seize him.

Meanwhile the people cried out and said, "What sin has Peter committed, or what harm has he caused you, O Agrippa?" You are hurt by something else. If he dies, we fear that Christ will exterminate us all."

But Peter entered into their midst and calmed them, saying to them: "Men who are designated to be the people of Our Lord! You men, whose hope is Jesus Christ, remember completely what miracles you have seen from me! Remember completely the powers of the Lord, how many healings Jesus Christ has done through me. Leave him alone, for he will come and reward everyone according to his works. Now do not be angry because of Agrippa, for he is his father's servant. He helps him, but this is what I have to bear, because my Lord revealed himself to me and told me what was going to happen to me. Do then, Agrippa, what you have in your heart or what you lead me to. It is my crucifixion."

And as soon as they brought him to the king, he began to pray and to speak: "O name of the mysterious and hidden cross! O ineffable grace given in the name of the cross! O nature therefore of man, who cannot distance himself from God! I force you, you who have arrived at the approach of eternal rest, to hear what I will not cease to reveal. The spirit of my breath calls me to the hidden mystery of the cross. Now, do not believe the cross as it seems dishonored, and do not believe it especially at the moment when you have the strength to hear, you who are capable of acting, because I find myself at the end of the last hour. I want to tell you the words of life. Listen, brethren, and gather them all into your hearts of understanding. All of you, purify your souls through the body that truly remains. Take your faces away from blindness and openly turn your hearts of understanding to me. Comment on what is visible and recognize what is done by Christ and the mystery of your life."

They said to him, "Well for you, Peter, the time has come to put your body in the hands of these warriors, for it is their business".

Saint Peter entered (among them) to be crucified and he said: "I beg you, you warriors, to believe me. Make it in this way, the head turns downwards and not in any other way, so that I am not comparable to my Lord".

And when they had hung him on the tree, he began to speak and he said: "Men, those who suit it, lend your ears, especially to what I have just told you, it is the mystery of all nature. The beginning of all creation is the first that was born. Now the first man who was made an image (of God) was hanged with his head turned downwards. This is what revealed the non-being of creation at that time, for it was dead, it certainly had no movement, it fell, it transformed its beginning into dust, unveiled all this spectacle of the universe, and knocked him down. He showed his left as the right and his right as they left. And he changed all the signs of nature - that good does not appear good to you, that good appears to you as evil and evil as good, and that is why the Lord said mysteriously: 'If you do not go right and left, and above and below, you shall not know the kingdom of God.' These thoughts, it is He who made them for me, and this image such as you see me was drawn by Him, it is that of the first man. Known since He first introduced the creation of man. And you, my beloved brethren, and those who have to hear it in the future and those who first fell to share this ordeal, you will then be worthy of climbing this mountain. For it is from reason that we expect the king, the Christ, to designate the unique and only Word, of whom the Holy Spirit said: 'What is Christ, if not the Word of God?' Otherwise, the tree above me, on which I am crucified, because moaning is reversed in the nature of Man. Now, the nail in the middle, which holds the body straight to the tree, is the conversion of man and his penance. It is you, Word of life, who taught me and revealed this tree, the subject of my discourse. I thank you. You, unique one, are not from this mouth of this passing low world, not from this language, from which both truth and lies come, not from this word which is composed by the art of this world."

"No, I thank you, You, Eternal King, who's voice is recognizable by its silence, which acts not by a material organ subject to corruption, which reaches not bodily hearing, which subsists not in this world, incapable to contain it, likewise it is not by inscription in a book, nor by anything unreal that I thank You, but I thank You, Lord Jesus Christ. By this voice, which is yours, this spirit subsisting in me which loves you and which preaches in your name. I appeal to You, who are recognizable only by spirit. You are my Father, you are my Mother, you are my Brother, you are my fighter, you are everything and everything is in You. There is no being which exists except you. Throw up to Him, my brothers! Learn how to direct yourself to Him alone! Ask Him for the things He promises to give you, what eyes have not seen and ears have not heard, what has not reached the human heart and what God has prepared for those whom He loves. I beg You, Christ, to grant me what You have promised me. I thank You, I confess and glorify You, for You are the one Lord and there is no other but You, and Yours is the glory from century to century. Amen".

And as soon as the numerous people who were present answered: "Amen!" With a deep sigh, the crucified thrice-blessed Peter gave up his Soul to the Lord. However, Marcel did not think he had to come back to the same mindset as Agrippa or with another who did not suit him. As soon as he heard that St. Peter was dead, he took him down from the cross with his own hands, washed him with milk and wine he crushed about fifty liters of chromium and aloes, and as many other aromatic leaves. He embalmed the body of St. Peter. He filled the chasm with virgin honey and placed it in his grave.

Now, Blessed Peterapp eared the same night in a vision and said to him: "Have you not heard, Marcel, this word of the Lord: 'Let the dead bury the dead!'" And Marcel answered: "Yes, sir, I heard it correctly".

Then Peter replied: "What you had, you lost for the dead, since you, the living, have it, such as a dead man that heals the dead". Marcel woke up and told his brothers all the revelation that Saint Peter had given him. He told it to all the brothers who were, and, thanks to Peter, firm in Our Lord Jesus Christ, they all held firm and these believers became even more fervent at the arrival of Paul in Rome.

Now, informed of Saint Peter's departure from this life, the Emperor Nero accused Agrippa, saying to him: "Why did you kill him without trial?" Not wishing to subject him to stronger torments, since Peter had made disciples of some people from Nero's suite, and he had separated them from him. This is why Nero was displeased, for a long time he took no advice from Agrippa and sought to exterminate all of St. Peter's followers.

He was tormented one night in his sleep by a person who appeared to him and said to him, "Nero, you cannot henceforth persecute the disciples of God and destroy them. Get your hands off them!" Nero was then afraid and refrained from persecuting the disciples of Our Lord Jesus Christ.

At that time, when Saint Peter had left this world, all the believers of Our Lord Jesus Christ gathered together and unanimously glorified the most honored and magnificent name of the Father, and of the Son and of the Holy Spirit, now and always and from age to age. Amen.

VIII. — THE MARTYRSHIP OF SAINT PAUL, APOSTLE AT ROME

In Rome, Luke was waiting for Paul of Galatia. Titus had come from Dalmatia. Paul saw them all and rejoiced. He abided in a store outside of Rome in which he lived with brothers, and he taught everyone the word of life. He welcomed and treated well all who came to him and he was celebrated by all in Rome.

Many people were won over to Our Lord and many of the Emperor's court wandered. It was a great joy for all. A cantor for the emperor, who was called Patroclus, came in the evening to Paul's residence. The multitude was so great that he could not penetrate inside. So he sat in a high window and listened to what Paul was teaching from the word of God. However, the devil who at first always envies the grace of the Lord, the love and the life of believers, plunged Patroclus into sleep, he fell from the third floor and died. The Emperor was immediately informed.

However, Saint Paul, enlightened by the Spirit, said to those who were listening to him: "My brothers, the evil one has found the place to put us to the test. Go out and find the young man who fell from the window and who is dead. Bring it here quickly!"

They went out and brought it to Paul. When the people saw this, they were troubled. Saint Paul said to them: "Now is the time to show your faith. Come all and pray to the Lord in tears so that this young man lives again and that we are all innocent." And when they came and sighed to God, the young man recovered his soul, thanks to Christ, and he got up. They put him on a mount and sent him to the emperor together with other people from the emperor's court.

At the announcement of the death of Patroclus, the emperor came out of the bath, for he was very grieved and ordered to name another cantor in the place of Patroclus. The servants said to him: "Lord Emperor, Patroclus is alive, he is at the door outside." Patroclus was afraid to enter the emperor.

And as soon as he entered, the emperor asked him: "Are you alive?" And he answered: "Yes, I am alive, Lord Emperor." The Emperor asked: "Who is the one who healed?" The young man, full of a heart inspired by faith, answered him: "It is Jesus Christ, Lord Eternal."

The emperor got angry and said to him: "How then, is it He who, from now on, will be emperor from century to century and will dominate all the kings?" Patroclus said to him: "Yes, emperor, for he will destroy all the kingdoms, and he will be the only king of kings and there will be no kingdom that will be spared." The emperor instantly struck him in the face and said to him: "Have you, Patroclus, also submitted yourself to the same king?"

"Yes, Lord," he replied, "for he has raised me up."

After that, Barsabbas, the son of Justus, Lurion of Cappadocia, and Festus of Galatia, who were followers of the Emperor Nero, they also replied and said to him: "We also believe in the same Lord."

So the emperor had them seized, imprisoned and had everyone he loved beaten. He ordered a search for the slaves of the so-called great king. He issued in letters the following ordinance: "To exterminate all those who are found to be Christians and of the Christian army." With many others they brought Paul, who was bound and whom all regarded as the object of their attachment. The emperor understood that he was the leader of this army.

The emperor said: "Man of the king, who is said to be great, why did you have the thought in your heart to come to the principality of the Romans and why are you gathering an army in my domains?"

Now, Paul, filled with the Holy Spirit, said to him in front of all the people: "It is not from your corner alone that we gather the army, but from all the universe, because Our Lord taught us to so: 'Do not hinder anyone who wants to become the soldier of the Eternal Lord.' Neither the wealth nor the splendor of this world will deliver you, for it is He, the man himself, who is the eternal King, Judge of the universe." At these words, the emperor became more and more furious. He ordered to burn all those who were present, except Paul whose head he ordered to be cut off according to Roman law.

Now Paul was not silent, but preached the words of God to them, to Iluleon, the chief commander of the army, and Questocles the centurion. Meanwhile, Emperor Nero was staying in Rome and busy arranging a lot of the devil's business. By his order, so many Christians were exterminated that all the Romans gathered at the imperial palace and shouted aloud, saying: "Enough is enough, emperor, for these men are ours and you are slaughtering the Roman people".

Then the Emperor Nero calmed his rage and gave the order: "Let no one deliver the Christians until I inquire into the truth concerning Paul". Then, following the order, Saint Paul was brought in the usual way to the Emperor Nero who had already condemned Paul to have his head cut off. Now, Paul said to him: "Emperor, it is not for a short duration that I will live by my Lord, and when you have cut off my head, I will rise again and I will reveal myself to you so that you know that I am not dead, but that I am alive, thanks to my Lord Jesus Christ who will come to judge the world".

Now, Longon and Questos said to him: "From where does this Lord come to you, in whom you believe to such a degree and whom you do not want to betray until death?"

Saint Paul said to them: "You other men, who find yourselves all in ignorance and the seductions of this world, convert yourselves and deliver yourselves from the fire to come. It is not that we are designed to be the army proper to an earthly king, as you think, but we are the army of the living and future God who has come into this world because of his impiety. And blessed will be everyone who believes in Him, for he will obtain eternal salvation". Now, Longon and Questos said to Paul, begging him: "We beg you, do us grace and restore us to the state in which you are, and we will give you freedom."

Saint Paul tells them: "I am not a deserter of Christ; I am a loyal soldier of the living God. If I had to die close to my God, I would have done as you tell me, you, Longon and Questos, but I am alive by God. I love him and I go to the Lord in order to come with Him, when He comes in the glory of the Father".

They said to him, "As soon as your head is cut off, we will be saved." At these words, the envoys of the Emperor Nero, a certain Ferentian and Patrinios, came to ascertain whether Paul's head was really cut off, and they found him alive.

Paul said to them, "Believe in the living God who is mine and of all those who have faith in Him, He who raises the dead". Now, they said: "Let us therefore go to the Emperor Nero, and when, once dead, you rise again, then we will believe in your God."

In the meantime, Longon and Questos prayed to Saint Paul for their salvation. Paul said to them: "Tomorrow, when you come to my tomb, you will find two men there praying, Titus and Luke, and they will confer the seal on you from God." As soon as Paul had said these words to them, he turned towards the East and prayed a long time before God with his hands stretched out towards heaven. And when he stopped praying, he suddenly exhorted everyone in general and he taught the word of life in Hebrew to all the brothers and fathers. Then Saint Paul joyfully stretched out his neck to the executioner's sword. And there, by the grace of God, suddenly sprang from Paul's neck milk instead of blood.

The clothes of the executioner were sprinkled with this milk and the executioner and all the multitude of the people who were present were astonished at the miracle. They glorified the God who bestowed such glory on blessed Paul. They then went to tell the Emperor Nero what had happened to Blessed Paul. At the announcement of this event, the Emperor Nero was very trepidatious. He thought for a long time about this miracle of Paul. Paul came exactly at nine o'clock, when he found himself in the presence of the emperor, many people, philosophers, centurions and friends.

And Saint Paul said aloud To the Emperor Nero: "Emperor, I am here, I, soldier of the living God. Believe then in me, for I am not dead, I am alive by my God, but for you, unhappy one, many anguishes and great torments are reserved for you, because you have shed a lot of innocent blood. And it will happen to you in a few days". Having said this, Paul rose up away from them. At this the Emperor was disturbed. He ordered all the prisoners to be freed and Patroclus and Barsabbas to go with their relatives. And as Saint Peter commanded them, Longo and Questos marched at dawn to the sepulcher, and they went towards him in fear.

When they got there, they found two men praying at the tomb, as Paul had told them, and in the midst of them Paul was standing. Seeing this glorious fact, their hearts were amazed. As for Titus and Luke, a great fear seized them and they began to flee. Longon and Questos pursued them, overtook them, and said to them, "It is not to assassinate you that we pursue you, as you believe, saintly men, happy with the living God, but that you may give us eternal life, as Saint Paul promised us, whom we saw a short time ago, standing in prayer in the midst of you".

Having heard this from these men, Titus and Luke returned with much joy and gaiety and conferred on them the seal of Christ, glorifying over all these facts. God the Father and Our Lord Jesus Christ who belongs the glory and the power with the Holy Spirit Now and always from century to century. Amen.

IX. — THE MARTYRDOM OF THE SAINTS AND MOST PRAISE APOSTLES PETER AND PAUL BY THE EMPEROR NERO AT ROME.

And it was at the time when Paul arrived from the island of the Ghamdumelites and wanted to come to Italy. The Jews, priests in the city of Rome, learned that Paul intended to come to the emperor. The concern and the dissatisfaction spread among them. They asked each other, "Is this not enough? For he single-handedly disturbed all our brothers and our relatives in Judea, Samaria, and Palestine. It is here that he now comes with deceitfulness to seek the emperor to destroy us". The Jews called a meeting about Paul, they deliberated, spoke gossip, and decided to go to the king, Nero who reigned then, so that they would prevent Paul from coming to Rome.

They had quickly prepared important gifts, took them and brought them to the king, saying: "We pray to you, mighty lord! Send prescriptions throughout your kingdom and order that a certain Paul be forbidden to enter Rome. It is this Paul who troubled our whole nation, the legacy of our ancestors, he now intends to come here even to destroy us. We have had enough, gracious king, just as the concern we had for Peter."

As soon as the kingNero heard this prayer, he answered them: "Let it be done according to your will. And I will insist in all the states of our domination that it does not cross the borders of Italy. While these were deliberating in this way, some pagans about to be converted and others enlightened by the teaching of Peter sent a messenger to Paul with a letter, in which was written the following: "Paul, faithful to our Lord Jesus Christ and brother of Peter, chief of the apostles, we have learned from the chiefs of the Jews who live in Rome, that they have requested the emperor to send envoys to all the states of his domination with orders to kill where you are found. In the meantime, we are convinced that like two well-known stars that God, Our Creator will not separate you from each other, neither Peter from Paul, nor Paul from the Rock. Now, we all believe together in Our Lord Jesus Christ, whose baptism we took, because we were worthy of your teaching."

And when these two men arrived on the 20th of May with the letter to St. Paul. He felt a new ardor within him and gave thanks to Our Lord Jesus Christ. Starting from the Ghavdomelites, he did not go from Africa, instead going towards the regions of Italy. He hastened to Sicily to go as far as the city of Syracuse, where he met these two men who had come from Rome to to seek him, and from there he went to Rigue of Caltane, and from Rigue he passed to Messina, where he ordained a bishop named Vacqulon. After leaving Messina, he came as far as Vidom, where he stayed one night, and from there he set out and arrived the following day at Pontius. Captain Dioscorus, who had brought him to Syracuse, did not leave Paul, because he had saved his son from death. He left his boat and followed it to Pontius. Peter's disciples were staying there and they welcomed Paul and begged him to stay with them. And he remained hidden there for a week because of the order of the emperor, because the patricians guarded all the places to seize him and kill him.

As for Captain Dioscorus, who had put on a purple coat and was bald, he was out walking the very day of his arrival with relaxed air, in the town of Pontius. It was believed that it was Paul, and they seized him, they cut off his head, which was sent to the emperor. The emperor summoned the authorities of the Jews and said to them: "Rejoice with great joy, because our enemy Paul is dead", and he showed them the head of Dioscorus. And there was great rejoicing on the same day, the 15th of June. All without exception erred that it was Paul whose head had been cut off.

However, Paul was living at Pontius, and when he learned that Dioscorus' head had been cut off, he was afflicted with great grief, he raised his gaze to heaven and said: "Almighty Lord, You who were present to me everywhere I walk, put yourself in the name of your Word, Our Lord Jesus Christ, in anger against this city! And he led away all those who wandered in God and followed his word.

Paul said to them, "Follow me! Paul, accompanied by those who wandered in the word of God, left Pontius and came to a place called Beas Everyone, immediately glancing back, saw the town of Pontius submerged near the shore of the sea, a depth of a phantom. And it remains under the sea until today in commemoration.

Leaving Beas, Paul entered Get, where he taught the word of God. He remained there three days in the house of Erastus, whom Peter had sent from Rome to teach the Gospel of God. Leaving Get, he went to the town called Taracinas. He stayed there for seven days in the house of Deaconess Cosaria, which Peter had consecrated. He crossed the river and came to the place called Tabernis.

And those who had fled from the submerged town of Pontius went to tell the Emperor of Rome that Pontius had been swallowed up with all its population. The emperor was very distressed because of the city and, when the authorities of the Jews were called, he said to them: "Look, I gave the order to kill Paul and it is because I listened to you that the city has become submerged".

And they said to the emperor: "Gracious Lord, we did not warn you that it was Paul who revolted against all the populations in the East and who overthrew our fathers. Gracious King, it is better that one man perish and not your whole kingdom, for otherwise Rome would suffer the same fate. Hearing these words, the king consoled himself.

Now Paul, having only stayed two days around Tarbenis, went to the place called Amphipolis. At night he fell asleep there and had a vision. Someone was seated on a golden seat, and, standing in front of him, numerous barbarians spoke to him: "Today I committed murder of a father by his son". And another said to him: "I caused the collapse of a house and the death of parents and sons". And others told him many other cruel things.

Another came to inform him: "I have prepared for fornication with the bishop Jovenal, whom Peter had ordered". Having heard all this in his sleep at the place called Amphipolis, Paul immediately sent to Rome some of those who had followed him from Pontius, to tell the bishop Jovenal what he had been upset about.

The following day, after having heard them, Jovenal went to prostrate himself in front of Peter, he wept with sighs and said to him: "I was close to failing". And he told the whole affair and he said to him: "I believe in him who is the star and on whom wait." Peter therefore said to him: "How can it be since he has finished the course of this life? Then Jovenal brought those whom Paul had sent to Peter, and they told him that he was alive and that he was coming and that he lived in Amphipolis. And Peter gave thanks to God and glorified him.

So Peter called the believers, his disciples, and sent them to Paul. To reach the surroundings of Tarbenis, one has to travel an eighteen-mile path to Brindisi. Seeing them, Paul gave thanks to our God Jesus Christ, he grew bold and walked towards us to the city called Aricia.

There were rumors in Rome that Paul, brother of Peter, was alive and coming. "Let him who believes in God rejoice with great joy". A great confusion arose among the Jews who came to Simon the magician and said to him, imploring him: "Report to the king that Paul is not dead, that he is alive and that he has come."

Now, Simon said to the Jews: "Whose head was that which was brought from Pontius to the emperor? Wasn't he also bald? And as soon as Paul came to Rome, the great city of Rome stirred, and great fear fell upon the Jews. They came to Paul and implored him, saying: "To the faith in which you are true, you must hold; for it is not fitting that being a Jew by faith and one of the Jews, you should be supposed to be master of the Gentiles and judge of the uncircumcised in their faith, when you have somewhere visited Peter who has apostatized his master, because his faith is only an obstacle and a curse for our religion".

Paul replied to them, "If his doctrine be true, we must submit to it until the testimony of the scriptures of the Jews." This and other similar things that Paul said to them. And they told Peter that Paul had come to Rome. He was transported with great joy and, getting up immediately, he went home.

As soon as they saw each other, they wept with joy, and they burst into tears in a long-lasting embrace. As soon as Paul had related to Peter all the events that had happened and the sufferings that he had endured, Peter told him how he was harassed by Simon the magician and all that he had suffered. And having said this, Peter departed at the approach of evening. Returning the next day, he found a multitude of Jews standing outside Paul's door.

And there was great confusion among the Jews, Christians and Gentiles, for the Jews said: "We are the chosen race of the Kingdom and we are of the tribe of the priesthood, friends of Abraham, of Isaac and of Jacob and of all the prophets whom God inspired and to whom He revealed the mystery and the greatest wonders.

"As for you who are pagans, your race is not great and you bow down before empty and carved idols". This is how the Jews spoke or approximately.

The pagans said: "As soon as we heard the truth, we immediately followed it, leaving our past seductions. It is you who have known the very power of the patriarchs, who have seen the miracles of the prophets, who have received the law, who have crossed the sea and seen your enemies swallowed up, it is to you who have appeared in the sky, at night, a cloud and a pillar of fire, it is you who received manna from heaven and it is for you that the water springs from the rock, and after all this, you made a calf and love the emptiness. Now we have seen no miracles and we have believed that he is the God whom you have forsaken through ungodliness". This is how they pleaded and in a similar way.

Paul the apostle said, "You need not such pleading, but rather to keep well what you have received, because God has fulfilled His promise, the one He made Abraham our father, to know that from his race shall come He who shall inherit from the pagans, for there is no partiality with God". At these words of Paul, the Jews and the Gentiles calmed down.

Other Titles by D.P. Curtin:

First Book of Ethiopian Maccabees (2018)
The Georgian Synaxarium (2022)
About Fifteen Problems (De quindecim problematibus) by Albertus Magnus (2022)
Instructions: Counsel for Novices by St. Ammonas the Hermit (2022)
The Syriac Menologium and Martyrology (2022)
Book on Religious Exercise and Quiet by St. Isaiah the Solitary (2022)
Vision of Theophilus by St. Cyril of Alexandria (2022)
On Fate (De Fato) by St. Albertus Magnus (2023)
Fragments of 'Chronicle' by Hippolytus of Thebes (2023)
Life of the Blessed Theotokos by Epiphanius Monachus (2023)
Syriac Life of John the Baptist by Serapion the Presbyter (2023)
Second Book of Ethiopian Maccabees (2023)

www.ingramcontent.com/pod-product-compliance
Lightning Source LLC
Chambersburg PA
CBHW051553120626
46551CB00013B/1500